PRESIDENTS OF A GROWING COUNTRY

A SOURCEBOOK ON THE U.S. PRESIDENCY

PRESIDENTS OF A GROWING COUNTRY

A SOURCEBOOK ON THE U.S. PRESIDENCY

Edited by Carter Smith

AMERICAN ALBUMS FROM THE COLLECTIONS OF

THE LIBRARY OF CONGRESS

THE MILLBROOK PRESS, *Brookfield, Connecticut*

Cover: *Benjamin Harrison and the election of 1888. Cover of* Judge *magazine, vol. 14, no. 351, July 7, 1888.*

Title Page: *"The City of Washington: Birds-Eye View from the Potomac—Looking North." Color print by Charles R. Parsons, published by Currier & Ives, 1880.*

Contents Page: *campaign poster for William Jennings Bryan, 1900.*

Back Cover: *"Samuel J. Tilden—Died, August 4, 1886." Lithograph from* Puck *magazine, 1886.*

Library of Congress Cataloging-in-Publication Data

Presidents of a growing country : a sourcebook on the U.S. presidency / edited
    by Carter Smith.
        p. cm. — (American albums from the collections of the Library of
Congress)
    Includes bibliographical references and index.
    Summary: Uses a variety of contemporary materials to describe and
illustrate the political and personal lives of the United States presidents from
Rutherford Hayes to William McKinley
        ISBN 1-56294-358-8 (lib. bdg.)
        1. Presidents—United States—History—19th century—Juvenile literature.
2. Presidents—United States—History—19th century—Sources—Juvenile
literature. 3. United States—Politics and government—1865–1900—Sources—
Juvenile literature. 4. United States—Politics and government—1865–1900—
Juvenile literature. [1. Presidents—Sources. 2. United States—Politics and
government—1865–1900—Sources.] I. Smith, C. Carter. II. Series.
E176.1.P926 1993
973.8'092—dc20
[B]   93-15090
                                                                                    CIP
                                                                                     AC

 Created in association with Media Projects Incorporated

C. Carter Smith, *Executive Editor*
Lelia Wardwell, *Managing Editor*
Charles A. Wills, *Principal Writer*
Elizabeth Prince, *Manuscript Editor*
Lydia Link, *Designer*
Athena Angelos, *Picture Researcher*
Shelley Latham, *Researcher*

The consultation of Bernard F. Reilly, Jr., Head Curator of the Prints and
Photographs Division of the Library of Congress, is gratefully acknowledged.

10 9 8 7 6 5 4 3 2 1

Contents

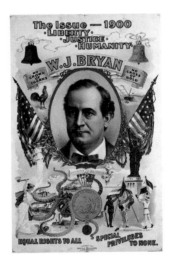

This lithograph depicts a model of the Washington Monument, built to honor the nation's first president, in Washington, D.C. (The colonnade at the monument's base, while shown here, was never actually built.) The cornerstone was laid on July 4, 1848, when James K. Polk was president, but the 555-foot-high structure wasn't completed until 1884, during Chester Arthur's administration.

Introduction

PRESIDENTS OF A GROWING COUNTRY is one of the volumes in a series published by The Millbrook Press titled AMERICAN ALBUMS FROM THE COLLECTIONS OF THE LIBRARY OF CONGRESS and one of six books in the series subtitled SOURCEBOOKS ON THE U.S. PRESIDENCY. This series chronicles the American presidency from George Washington through Bill Clinton.

The prints, banners, magazine illustrations, manuscripts, and other ephemera reproduced in this volume reflect the extraordinary wealth of the Library's holdings of presidential documents. In fact, Thomas Jefferson's personal library formed the basis of the Library of Congress after the institution's original collections were burned by British troops during the War of 1812. Established long before the first presidential library, the Library of Congress also houses the papers of every American president from George Washington to Calvin Coolidge. These papers are supplemented in many instances by the personal memorabilia of the presidents, including photographs, prints, and drawings.

Many of the works shown here are political cartoons from *Puck*, *Judge*, and the other satirical weeklies and illustrated newspapers that flourished during the late nineteenth century. From the Civil War on, the national press widely incorporated illustrations and cartoons to augment written news coverage and political commentary. The public appetite for images of the battlefields of Virginia, Maryland, and farther South during the Civil War convinced editors of the enduring appeal of pictorial journalism. The leading illustrated magazine, *Harper's Weekly*, pioneered the assignment of the artists to the field and the rapid publications of their "eyewitness" drawings. *Puck* and *Judge*, two satirical magazines founded in the1870s, filled their pages with comic drawings and lively commentary. Essentially, they rendered the individually-issued cartoon obsolete.

The works reproduced here provide varied perspectives on the presidency through the years. They are a small but telling portion of the rich record of the American presidency, which is preserved today by the Library of Congress in its role as the nation's library.

BERNARD F. REILLY, JR.

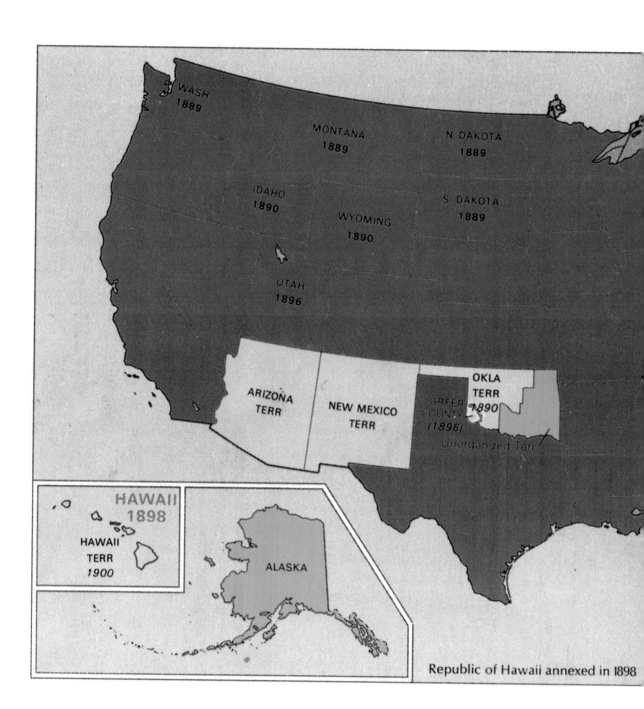

WASH 1889

MONTANA 1889

N DAKOTA 1889

IDAHO 1890

S DAKOTA 1889

WYOMING 1890

UTAH 1896

OKLA TERR 1890

ARIZONA TERR

NEW MEXICO TERR

GREER COUNTY (1896)

Unorganized Terr

HAWAII 1898

HAWAII TERR 1900

ALASKA

Republic of Hawaii annexed in 1898

1900

The years from 1876 to 1901 were a time of great growth for the United States—both within its continental borders and beyond them.

The great age of Western settlement finally ended during this era. Seven Western states were admitted to the Union during the 1880s and 1890s, six of them (North Dakota, South Dakota, Montana, Washington, Idaho, and Wyoming) while Benjamin Harrison was president. The seventh, Utah, won admission during Grover Cleveland's second administration. By 1890, most of the region's Native Americans were crowded onto reservations. In the late 1880s and early 1890s, the area once set aside as a permanent Indian Territory was also opened to white settlement and organized as the Oklahoma Territory. Arizona and New Mexico were also U.S. territories at this time.

With the West settled, some Americans began to call for the nation to expand beyond the Atlantic and Pacific coasts. When American business people toppled the native government of Hawaii in 1893, many Americans, including President Benjamin Harrison, favored annexing the islands to the United States. This was finally achieved in 1898, and the islands were organized into a U.S. territory in 1900. (Alaska, purchased in 1867, was still unorganized territory.)

The Spanish-American War of 1898 fulfilled the dreams of those who wanted an American empire overseas. The treaty that ended the war transferred Puerto Rico in the West Indies and Guam in the Pacific to the United States, along with the Philippine Islands. By the turn of the century, the United States was the most powerful nation in the Western hemisphere.

A TIMELINE OF MAJOR EVENTS
1876–1882

THE PRESIDENCY

1876 Democrat Samuel Tilden receives about 250,000 more popular votes than Republican Rutherford B. Hayes in the presidential election. The Republicans dispute the results in the Electoral College and a special commission is set up to resolve the election. The Commission declares Hayes the winner.

1877 President Hayes orders the last federal troops stationed in the South to be withdrawn, ending Reconstruction.
• After strikes by railroad workers halt trains around the country, President Hayes sends federal troops to trouble spots to restore order.

1879 President Hayes vetoes a bill designed to limit immigration from

Protest in San Francisco against Chinese labor

China. California has already adopted a new state constitution prohibiting businesses from employing Chinese workers.

1880 The Republicans nominate Ohio governor James Garfield for president; the Democrats nominate former Civil War general Winfield Scott Hancock. Garfield wins the election by only 7,000 popular votes. (The Electoral College

THE AMERICAN SCENE

1877 After a four-month campaign, U.S. troops force the surrender of Chief Joseph, leader of a band of Nez Perce Indians who resisted removal from their Oregon homeland.

1878 The Knights of Labor, the first labor group to organize on a national scale, holds its first assembly in Philadelphia.
• Labor organizations join advo-

cates of paper money to form the Greenback-Labor Party. Its candidates capture more than 10 percent of the popular vote in the congressional elections.
• Yellow fever sweeps through the South during the summer. In New Orleans alone, 4,000 people die.
• In Missouri, Hungarian immigrant Joseph Pulitzer begins publishing his first newspaper,

the *St. Louis Post-Dispatch.*

1879 Congress passes an act allowing female lawyers to argue before the Supreme Court.
• Merchant Frank W. Woolworth opens his first "5-and-10-cent" store in Utica, New York. By 1910, Woolworth will be operating more than 1,000 stores around the nation.
• At his laboratory in Menlo Park, New Jersey, inventor Thomas Edison

demonstrates his incandescent light bulb. Patented the following year, Edison's electric light is soon in commercial use.

1880 The census finds that the population of the U.S. now stands at more than 50 million people. New York City is the first American city to have a population of more than one million.
• The National Farmer's Alliance is formed in Chicago to unite farmers

tally, however, was 214 to 155 in favor of Garfield.)
• Among the third-party candidates in the election of 1880 is Neal Dow, nominee of the National Prohibition Party. The party, founded in 1869, is the political arm of a growing movement to ban the sale of alcoholic beverages in the U.S.

1881 James Garfield is inaugurated as the nation's twentieth president.
• President Garfield directs Secretary of the Treasury William Windom to refund the national debt by calling in outstanding U.S. bonds and giving holders the option of cashing them or holding them at a lower interest rate.

July 2 Charles Guiteau shoots and seriously wounds President Garfield in a Washington railroad station. Garfield dies in September and Vice President Chester Arthur is sworn in as the nation's twenty-first president.
• President Arthur signs a bill authorizing the construction of four armor-plated warships, in order to strengthen the navy.
• After moving into the White House, President Chester Arthur discovers that the presidential mansion is suffering from decades of neglect. Arthur has twenty-four wagon loads of old furniture removed and orders both the public and private areas of the White House completely redecorated.

1882 After President Arthur vetoes an act that would prohibit Chinese laborers from entering the U.S. for twenty years, Congress passes the Chinese Exclusion Act. This legislation reduces the term of prohibition to ten years.
• Congress authorizes pensions of $5,000 per year for widows of presidents.

against discriminatory legislation.
• The American branch of the Salvation Army is established in Pennsylvania. The organization, founded in England in 1865, soon wins a widespread following in the United States.
• Inventor George Eastman patents the first practical roll film for cameras in Rochester, New York, making photography accessible to most Americans.

1881 In *Springer* v. *Illinois*, the Supreme Court declares the federal income tax (established in 1862) to be unconstitutional.
• Author Helen Hunt Jackson publishes *A Century of Dishonor*, a critical look at federal policy toward Native Americans. The book spurs a movement for reform in Indian affairs.
• The American Red Cross is estab-lished with veteran Civil War nurse Clara Barton as its first president.
• African-American educator Booker T. Washington founds the Tuskegee Institute in Alabama.
• Thomas Edison constructs the first electric power plant in the United States on Pearl Street in New York City.

1882 The Senate approves the Geneva Convention, providing care of the wounded during wartime.

Clara Barton

A TIMELINE OF MAJOR EVENTS
1883–1889

THE PRESIDENCY

1883 President Arthur signs the Pendleton Civil Service Act into law. The law's purpose is to ensure that civil service jobs are given out on the basis of ability and experience, not as political favors.

1884 Supporters of women's suffrage establish the National Equal Rights party and nominate Belva Lockwood for president.

• In one of the most bitter presidential elections in American history, Democrat Grover Cleveland defeats Republican James G. Blaine by a narrow margin.

1885 Grover Cleveland is inaugurated as the nation's twenty-second president.
• President Cleveland dedicates the Statue of Liberty, a gift of the people of France to the United States,

Tickertape parade supporting Cleveland

in New York Harbor.
• President Cleveland asks the Congress to set up a special commission to oversee

labor disputes.
• Congress passes the Presidential Succession Act. The law calls for the secretary of state to assume the presidency in the event that both the president and vice president die while still in office.
• To enforce an act of Congress passed earlier in the year, President Cleveland orders all illegal private enclosures, such as fences, to be removed from federally owned land in the Western states

THE AMERICAN SCENE

1883 The Supreme Court narrowly overturns the Civil Rights Act of 1873, which had outlawed racial segregation in "public accommodations" such as trains and restaurants.
• The Brooklyn Bridge is completed after thirteen years of construction. At 1,600 feet, it is the longest suspension bridge in the world.
• Former Western scout William "Buffalo Bill" Cody introduces his

famous "Wild West Show" in Platte, Nebraska. The wildly popular exhibition will give performances all over the world in the decades ahead.
• To resolve scheduling problems and provide more efficient service, railroads in Canada and the U.S. establish a system of standard time.

1884 The Supreme Court makes attempting to inter-

fere with a person's right to vote a federal offense. The case was brought by Southern blacks who had been prevented from voting by the Ku Klux Klan.
• Mark Twain's classic novel, *The Adventures of Huckleberry Finn*, is published.

1885 The Washington Monument, in Washington, D.C. is finally finished. (The monument took almost four decades to complete.)

1886 A bomb kills seven policemen as they attempt to break up a labor rally in Chicago's Haymarket Square. Despite a lack of solid evidence, eight labor activists are convicted of the crime; seven of them are sentenced to death.
• After years of fighting in the Southwest, Apache leader Geronimo and his band of warriors surrender to U.S. troops in the Arizona Territory.

and territories. The action is intended to halt the growing practice, by railroads and other commercial interests, to use public land for private profit.

1886 *The Personal Memoirs of U. S. Grant* are published after Grant's death from cancer. The work is a critical and commercial success, and its sales rescue the nearly bankrupt ex-president's family from the prospect of poverty.

• President Cleveland marries Frances Folsom, the daughter of a former law partner, in an evening ceremony in the White House.

1887 President Cleveland signs a congressional act establishing the Interstate Commerce Commission to regulate the activities of the railroads.
• In his annual message to Congress, President Cleveland gives an impas-

sioned speech in favor of reducing tariffs on foreign goods to bolster the economy. The speech focuses national attention on the issue.
• In order to avoid another disputed election like the one in 1876, Congress passes the Electoral Count Act. The law makes each state the final authority on its own election returns, and requires Congress to accept each state's results without question.

1888 Grover Cleveland receives 100,000 more popular votes than Republican Benjamin Harrison in the presidential election, but loses to him in the Electoral College.

1889 Benjamin Harrison is inaugurated as the nation's twenty-third president. Harrison, grandson of William Henry Harrison, is the only grandson of a president to become chief executive himself.

Riot in Chicago's Haymarket Square

1887 Several labor groups band together to create the American Federation of Labor in Columbus, Ohio. The AFL will become the nation's largest and most influen-

tial labor group.
• Congress passes the Dawes Severalty Act. The law, which divides reservation lands among Indian families, is an attempt to compensate Native Americans

for territories seized during westward expansion.

1888 A devastating blizzard blankets the East Coast with snow. The storm claims 400 lives in New York City alone. Property damage is considerable along the coast. Normal train and telegraph service takes weeks to be restored.

1889 About 2 million acres of land, formerly owned by Indian tribes in present-day

Oklahoma, are opened to white settlement.
• Thousands of settlers surge into the area in the first of several Oklahoma "land rushes."
• A dam break on the Conemaugh River unleashes a massive flood on Johnstown, Pennsylvania. More than 2,000 people are killed in one of the worst disasters in American history.

A TIMELINE OF MAJOR EVENTS
1890–1895

THE PRESIDENCY

1890 At Harrison's urging, Congress passes the Dependent and Disability Pension Act, which provides pensions for all veterans who are unable to perform manual labor, regardless of the cause of their disability.

1891 The Populist Party is organized in Cincinnati, Ohio. The party favors increased coinage of silver, which it believes will make credit

Settlers emigrating to Oklahoma camp for the night

easier to obtain and thus boost the lagging economy of the rural West.
• Angered by the Chilean government's slow investigation of a saloon brawl in Valparaiso, Chile, in which two American soldiers were killed and seventeen injured, President Harrison orders the navy to prepare for war. The crisis ends when a Chilean minister publicly apologizes for the incident.

1892 Harrison opens 3 million acres of Cheyenne and Arapaho land in Oklahoma to white settlers.
• Democrat and former president Grover Cleveland defeats Republican Benjamin Harrison in a landslide. Populist James B. Weaver receives more than one million votes.
• First Lady Caroline Harrison dies of tuberculosis, just two weeks

THE AMERICAN SCENE

1890 Congress passes the Sherman Antitrust Act. The law is aimed at curbing the power of the trusts—huge corporate monopolies able to fix prices by forcing smaller competitors out of business.
• U.S. troops massacre more than 100 Sioux Indians near Wounded Knee, South Dakota; two-thirds of the casualties are women and children.

• The National Women's Suffrage Association is formed in an effort to win women the right to vote in national elections.
• The census finds that the population of the U.S. is nearing 63 million. The rapid growth is due in part to increased immigration—more than a half-million immigrants arrive in 1890 alone.

1891 Using a soccer ball and two fruit baskets, college professor James Naismith invents the game of basketball in Springfield, Massachusetts.
• Massachusetts mechanics Charles and Frank Duryea build the first gasoline-powered automobile in the United States.

1892 Ellis Island in New York Harbor replaces Castle Garden as the nation's receiving point for immigrants. Between 1892 and 1954, more than 20 million people will pass through Ellis Island.
• Poet Walt Whitman publishes the final edition of his masterpiece, *Leaves of Grass*.
• In an influential speech titled "The Significance of the Frontier in American History," historian Frederick Jackson Turner claims that the frontier line, which has moved westward since colonial times, disappeared in 1890, signaling the end of westward expansion.

before the presidential election.

1893 A revolution led by American merchants overthrows Hawaiian queen Liliuokalani. Despite growing U.S. interest in annexing Hawaii, President Cleveland will not recognize the new Hawaiian Republic until July 1894.
• Grover Cleveland takes the oath of office. He is the first president to serve two non-consecutive terms.
• President Cleve-land opens the World's Columbian Exposition in Chicago. The fair, which features the products of American farms and factories and many international exhibits, celebrates the four-hundredth anniversary of Columbus's first voyage (actually completed in 1492).
• In an attempt to revive the floundering economy, President Cleveland calls an extra session of Congress to repeal the Sherman Silver Purchase Act. The repeal of the Act, which keeps the nation on the gold standard, is a blow to "bimetallists," who want more silver in circulation.

1894 After workers at the Pullman railroad car plant in Chicago strike to protest a cut in wages, the American Railway Union strikes in support, bringing trains to a halt throughout the Midwest. President Cleveland sends federal troops to restore order, and the strike disbands.
• After a border dispute erupts between Venezuela and British Guiana, President Cleveland warns Britain that any British occupation of Venezuelan territory will be seen as a violation of the Monroe Doctrine. The dispute, which looks as though it may lead to an Anglo-American war, is eventually settled peacefully.

1893 Steep drops in the New York Stock Exchange in May and June lead to a widespread economic slump. By the beginning of 1894, more than 2.5 million Americans are out of work.
• The Anti-Saloon League is founded in Oberlin, Ohio. This group and several others lobby for Prohibition—a government ban on the sale of alcohol.
• Bicycling becomes enormously popular with Americans,

Bicycling

both as a means of transportation and as a sport. By the end of the year, more than 1 million bicycles are in use in the United States.
• More than 1,000 people are killed when a fierce cyclone devastates Charleston, South Carolina, and Savannah, Georgia. Another 200 people die after another tropical storm hits coastal Louisiana in October.

1894 In a protest against the ongoing hard times, businessman Jacob Coxey leads an "army" of about 400 unemployed workers from Massilon, Ohio, to Washington, D.C.
• Congress establishes Labor Day as a national holiday.

1895 Novelist Stephen Crane publishes *The Red Badge of Courage*, a realistic novel about the Civil War.
• The first professional football game in U.S. history is played at Latrobe, Pennsylvania.
• The popular patriotic song *"America the Beautiful,"* by Katherine Lee Bates, is published.

A TIMELINE OF MAJOR EVENTS
1896–1901

THE PRESIDENCY

1896 Spain's refusal of President Cleveland's offer to act as a mediator in the bloody Cuban uprising against Spanish rule increases American sympathy for the Cuban rebels; American sympathy has already been fanned by grisly (and often untrue) reports of Spanish atrocities.
• After taking the Democratic convention by storm with his brilliant "Cross of Gold" speech advocating the free coinage of silver, William Jennings Bryan wins the nomination.
• Former Ohio governor William McKinley gets the Republican nomination at the party's June convention. McKinley's candidacy is supported by major corporations and newspapers, and he wins by a margin of more than a million popular votes.

1897 William McKinley is inaugurated as the nation's twenty-fifth president.

1898 On President McKinley's recommendation, Congress annexes Hawaii.
• While visiting Havana, the U.S. warship *Maine* explodes, killing 266 Americans. Although the cause of the explosion is unknown, the incident leads to more calls for war with Spain. McKinley ignores this outcry and attempts to solve the problem through legal means.
• When negotiations with Spain break down, President McKinley asks Congress to declare war.

1899 Filipino rebels attack U.S. troops in Manila. President McKinley orders the insurrection suppressed, beginning a bloody three-year struggle.
• The Treaty of Paris ends the Spanish-American War. At President

THE AMERICAN SCENE

1896 In *Plessy* v. *Ferguson*, the Supreme Court rules that "separate but equal" facilities for blacks and whites are constitutional.
• Gold is discovered near the Klondike River in the Yukon region of Alaska and northwestern Canada. Within two years, 25,000 fortune-seekers will arrive in the area.
• American athletes win nine of twelve events in the first modern Olympic Games, held in Athens, Greece.
• Richard Outcault's *"The Yellow Kid,"* the first newspaper comic strip, makes its appearance in the *New York World*.

April 23 The first public showing of motion pictures takes place in Koster & Bial's

Panning for gold in California

Music Hall in New York City.

June 4 Working in a shed behind his Detroit home, mechanic Henry Ford completes his first automobile. Although Ford is not the first American to develop a practical automobile, he goes on to become the nation's foremost automobile manufacturer.

1897 The first successful subway system in the U.S. opens in Boston.

McKinley's insistence, Cuba is granted independence, and Spain gives the Philippines, Puerto Rico, and Guam to the United States.

• Vice President Garrett A. Hobart dies in office, leaving the nation without a vice president until the election of Theodore Roosevelt in 1900.

• Congress approves the use of voting machines, rather than hand-marked ballots, in future presidential elections.

W. J. Bryan poster

1900 In the election of 1900, the candidates are the same as in 1896: Republican William McKinley and Democrat William Jennings Bryan. Despite an energetic campaign by Bryan, McKinley easily wins re-election.

• After Congress formally organizes newly-annexed Hawaii as a U.S. territory, President McKinley names Sanford B. Dole as the territory's first governor.

1901 William McKinley is sworn in for a second term.

• Although scattered resistance to U.S. rule in the Philippines will continue for years, President McKinley announces that the conflict between U.S. troops and Filipino guerrillas is at an end.

• President McKinley is shot and killed by anarchist Leon Czolgosz at the American Exhibition in Buffalo, New York.

• Vice President Theodore Roosevelt is sworn in as the nation's twenty-sixth president. At 42, he is the nation's youngest president ever.

The two-mile-long line operates below Tremont Street.

1898 After the end of the Spanish American War, it is found that only about 10 percent of the nearly 2,500 American deaths resulted from combat. The rest were due to disease caused by Cuba's tropical climate, which was made worse by the War Department's lack of preparation.

1899 The Automobile Club of America opens its first car show in New York City. There are only about 8,000 cars in the entire country at this time.

1900 The census puts the population of the U.S. at nearly 76 million.

• A massive hurricane rips through the city of Galveston, Texas, killing more than 6,000 people and destroying $20 million worth of property.

• A new baseball division, the American League, is founded in Chicago. The American League will not be recognized by the established National League until 1903.

• The Eastman Kodak Company begins selling the "Brownie" box camera. The Brownie, the first small, inexpensive, easy-to-operate camera, introduces amateur photography as a national hobby.

1901 The U.S. and Britain sign the Hay-Pauncefote Treaty, giving the United States the right to build and operate a canal across the isthmus of Panama.

• Anthony Lucas strikes oil at his spindletop well near Beaumont, Texas. With oil becoming more important as a fuel with the growth of the automobile, Texas and other oil-rich parts of the Southwest experience rapid economic growth.

VOL. IV.–No. 104.   MARCH 5, 1879.   Price, 10 Cents.

"What fools these Mortals be!"
MIDSUMMER-NIGHTS DREAM.

Puck

PUBLISHED BY
KEPPLER & SCHWARZMANN.
NEW YORK
TRADE MARK REGISTERED 1878.
OFFICE Nº 13 NORTH WILLIAM ST.

THE PRESIDENT'S DUTY.*

Hayes: "Veto!" — Kearney: "Then I'll secede!" — Hayes: "Then, I'll veto that, too!"

*) Our map of the Great United States and the little California is slightly different from the maps usually published.

Part I
The Presidency in the Gilded Age

When President Rutherford B. Hayes took office in 1877, more than 100,000 Chinese had immigrated to the United States. Congress quickly passed a bill forbidding Chinese laborers to enter the country, which Hayes vetoed. Hayes is shown in this Puck *magazine cartoon vetoing the "anti-Chinese bill" while Dennis Kearney, leader of San Francisco's "Workingman's Party" and opponent of Chinese immigration, threatens to "secede."*

The presidents of the later decades of the nineteenth century are among the nation's least-known chief executives. Twentieth-century writer Thomas Wolfe dubbed them "the lost Americans." They were a reflection of the times. Philosopher and historian Henry Adams, the grandson of one president and the great-grandson of another, wrote of this era: "No period so thoroughly ordinary had been known in American politics since Christopher Columbus first disturbed American society."

The nation did experience many changes in this era, including the settlement of the West, growing immigration, rising tension between labor and business, and the movement for women's rights. But the presidents who served from 1876 to 1889—Rutherford Hayes, James Garfield, Chester Arthur, and Grover Cleveland—played little or no part in these events. They were concerned mostly with the day-to-day business of government—improving the economy, dealing with Congress, and trying to push back the tide of corruption that swamped American politics in the years after the Civil War.

These "lost Americans" also shared similar backgrounds. Except for Grover Cleveland, all were Republicans. Hayes and Garfield grew up in Ohio; Arthur and Cleveland were New Yorkers. All (again, except for Cleveland) took part in the Civil War. And all four generally shared a limited view of the presidency's role in national life. Not until the last decade of the century would the presidency begin to take on the power and influence it has today.

RUTHERFORD HAYES: EARLY YEARS

Rutherford Birchard Hayes was born in Delaware, Ohio, on October 4, 1822, ten weeks after the death of his father, a local merchant. As a child, Rutherford was sick so often that his mother feared that he, too, would die, but he grew into an intelligent young man with a sense of humor and a stubborn, cautious temperament.

Two people greatly influenced young Hayes. The first was his mother, Sophia Birchard Hayes, a devout Methodist who passed on her strong religious beliefs to her son. The second was his uncle, Sardis Birchard, who became very much like a father to Rutherford. Thanks to Birchard, Hayes received a first-class education.

After attending private prep schools in Ohio and Connecticut, Hayes entered Kenyon College in Gambier, Ohio. Graduating in 1843, Hayes went on to study at Harvard Law School. After winning admission to the bar in 1845, Hayes began practicing law in partnership with his uncle. Four years later he settled in Cincinnati and opened his own practice.

In 1847, Hayes met Lucy Webb, the daughter of a Fremont, Ohio, doctor. Lucy was sixteen at the time—"not quite old enough to fall in love with," Hayes wrote. When he moved to Cincinnati in 1849, Hayes found that Lucy was attending college in the city. After a three-year courtship, the two were married on December 30, 1852.

Lucy Webb posed for this portrait (above) as a sixteen-year-old student at Ohio Wesleyan College. She became the first wife of a U.S. president to hold a college degree. Although Lucy Hayes avoided political discussions, many Americans believed she often told the president what to do. "In the absence of his wife," reported a newspaper when Lucy took a trip to Ohio without Rutherford, "Mr. Hayes is acting president."

This 1876 photograph (right) depicts the Delaware, Ohio, birthplace of Rutherford Hayes. Neighbors recalled "Rud," as young Hayes was nicknamed, as a well-mannered boy. His classmates at the Methodist Academy in nearby Norwalk, Ohio, remembered him as the school's champion speller.

President Hayes is flanked by sons James Webb Hayes (1856–1934; at left) and Birchard Austin Hayes (1853–1926; at right) in this photograph taken in the late 1870s. Rutherford and Lucy Hayes had eight children in all, three of whom died before reaching adulthood.

LEADER IN WAR AND PEACE

Lucy and Rutherford Hayes were a good match in many ways. Both were intelligent and deeply religious people. But while Rutherford was cautious and conservative, Lucy was a strong supporter of causes that were considered radical at the time—including women's rights and abolitionism (the movement to end slavery). At Lucy's urging, Hayes entered the struggle against slavery. In court, Hayes used his legal skills to keep runaway slaves in Ohio from being returned to the South. He also joined the Republican Party, which opposed the spread of slavery. In 1858, he entered politics as city solicitor (lawyer) for Cincinnati.

The Civil War put Hayes's political career on hold. Two months after the Confederate attack on Fort Sumter, he was commissioned a major in a regiment of Ohio volunteers. The Cincinnati lawyer turned out to be a brave soldier and an excellent officer. Hayes fought in many battles, was wounded twice, and ended the war as a major general.

Thanks to his war record, Hayes was elected to the House of Representatives before the end of the fighting. He finally took his seat in December 1865. In 1868, Hayes returned to Ohio to serve two terms as governor. In 1872, he left the governorship to run for Congress again, but was defeated. Three years later Hayes won a third term as governor.

Hayes's uniform bears the single star of a brigadier general in this October 1864 portrait (right). Hayes was proud of his Civil War service and liked to be called "the General" even after he became governor of Ohio and president of the United States. "I am more gratified by references to my war record," he wrote after leaving the White House, "than by any other flattery."

At the battle of South Mountain, Maryland, in September 1862, Hayes, then a lieutenant colonel, led his regiment in an uphill assault on a strongly held Confederate position. One third of the regiment fell during the attack, and Hayes himself suffered a serious wound in his left arm. This lithograph (below) shows the charge of the Ohio Volunteers against the North Carolina regiments. On both sides, more than 4,500 soldiers were killed or wounded in the battle.

THE ELECTION OF 1876

The Republican Party faced a challenge as the election year of 1876 approached. Most of the former Confederate states, which had largely Democratic voting populations, were now back in the Union. For the first time in four presidential elections, the number of Democratic and Republican voters would be roughly equal.

Also, the many scandals of Republican president Ulysses S. Grant's administration put the party in a bad light. To win, the Republicans believed they needed a candidate with a reputation for honesty. They also wanted a candidate with a good war record to appeal to the many voters who were veterans of the Union armies.

At the party convention, held in Cincinnati in June 1876, the Republicans finally found a candidate who fit the bill—Rutherford B. Hayes. At first, the Ohio governor wasn't a contender for the nomination. After the party failed to agree on a candidate after six ballots, Hayes finally won the nomination. Hayes accepted and chose New York Representative William A. Wheeler as his running mate.

The Democrats, meeting in St. Louis a few days later, nominated New York governor Samuel J. Tilden. Like Hayes, Tilden had a reputation as an honest politician in an era of widespread corruption. It was a close race, and when the votes were counted it looked like defeat for Hayes and the Republicans.

"Tilden and Reform" was one of the Democratic campaign slogans in 1876. The Democrats pointed to the corruption in Republican Ulysses S. Grant's administration as proof that the White House needed a change of party. This Democratic campaign poster (above) features the figure of a woman emerging from a sinking ship of state bearing a banner labeled "Reform."

Shown as it appeared in the election year of 1876 is Spiegel Grove in Fremont, Ohio—home to the Hayes family from 1873 to 1893 (right). Originally a simple brick house built in 1859 by Hayes's uncle, Sardis Birchard, the structure was expanded into a twenty-room house during the early 1870s.

Currier & Ives's "Grand National Republican Banner" (right) for 1876 includes portraits of Hayes and his running mate, William A. Wheeler. Republican campaign literature reminded voters that many Democrats had supported the Confederacy during the Civil War. According to one observer, the Republicans liked to point out that "not every Democrat was a Rebel [Confederate], but every Rebel was a Democrat."

THE "STOLEN ELECTION"

In the popular vote, the count for Tilden was roughly 4.3 million—about 250,000 more votes than Hayes received. In the Electoral College the margin was razor-thin. Tilden had 184 votes—one vote less than he needed to claim victory at that time.

Twenty electoral votes, however, were in dispute. All but one of them came from Florida, Louisiana, and South Carolina—ex-Confederate states still under military occupation by federal troops. For these states, there were two sets of election returns—one favoring each candidate. Each side charged the other with voter fraud. Not only was there no clear winner, but the Constitution contained no specific rules on how to resolve a dispute of this kind.

After weeks of debate in Congress, a special electoral commission, made up of equal numbers of senators, representatives, and Supreme Court justices, formed to determine which set of returns to accept. It was supposed to include seven Democrats, seven Republicans, and one independent member. But in early 1877, the independent commissioner was replaced by a Supreme Court justice who sided with the Republicans. When the commission finally voted, the count was 8 to 7 in favor of the Republican version of the returns. At 4:00 a.m. on the morning of March 2, 1877, the commission declared Hayes the nineteenth president of the United States.

This 1879 painting by Cornelia Fassett shows the Electoral
Commission discussing the disputed election returns in the
Senate chamber. The fifteen members of the commission sit on the
raised platform at left, while the gallery and floor are crowded
with journalists, politicians, lawyers, and visitors. Among the
commission's Republican members was Representative James
Garfield of Ohio, who would succeed Hayes as president.

This engraving (above) shows the Electoral Commission meeting by candlelight toward the end of the election controversy, in March 1877. The commission announced its decision March 2. On Saturday, March 3, Hayes took the oath of office in a private ceremony at the White House. The swearing-in was repeated in public at the Capitol on March 5.

Tilden urged his angry supporters to accept the commission's decision peacefully, for the good of the country. This Puck illustration (right) shows Tilden refusing to accept the flaming torch of "insurrection" (violent rebellion), while the members of the Electoral Commission look on.

A pro-Tilden cartoon (right) shows Hayes advancing to the "presidential chair" across a field of bayonets. This refers to the federal troops that still occupied ex-Confederate states. The words on Hayes's balancing pole—"Minority" and "Grantism"—refer to Hayes's lack of a majority in the popular vote, and to the corruption of the Grant administration.

HAYES AND THE END OF RECONSTRUCTION

Before the commission announced its decision, Democrats in Congress believed that Hayes would be named the winner. They agreed to accept Hayes as president only if the Republicans met certain conditions. In a series of secret meetings, Republican and Democratic leaders worked out a deal. In return for accepting Hayes, the new president would withdraw the last federal troops from Louisiana and South Carolina and support more federal spending on the Southern states. Although it was not officially part of the bargain, the Democrats wanted the new president to end enforcement of the Reconstruction laws passed after the Civil War.

These laws were passed to protect the civil rights of the more than 2 million slaves freed by the war. Many white Southern Democrats hated the laws and wanted Reconstruction to end. They got their wish. A few weeks after the new president took office, the last troops left the South. Hayes hoped the Southern state governments would continue to respect the rights of their black citizens, but he was disappointed. In 1878, Hayes said, "I am reluctantly forced to admit that the experiment [Reconstruction] was a failure."

By the end of Hayes's presidency, African Americans in the South had lost most of the rights gained during Reconstruction. They would not recover them for almost a century.

This lithograph (above) shows Rutherford and Lucy Hayes as they looked during Hayes's presidency. Many Democrats, angry over the disputed election, gave the new president several unflattering nicknames—"His Fraudulency," or "Rutherfraud B. Hayes," among others.

A hopeful engraving (below) shows Hayes reuniting the North and South after the bitterness of the Civil War and Reconstruction. Thanks to his withdrawal of federal troops from the South and other concessions, tensions between the two sections of the country did ease during Hayes's presidency. For the South's former slaves, however, Hayes's presidency marked the loss of their newly won political and civil rights.

RUTHERFORD HAYES: LATER YEARS

Rutherford Hayes's presidency was very different from that of his predecessor, Ulysses S. Grant. Scandal after scandal broke out during Grant's two terms; there were none in Hayes's White House. At Lucy Hayes's urging, the president banned alcohol from the White House—leading one reporter to describe a state dinner as "a brilliant affair; the water flowed like champagne." Other reporters dubbed the First Lady "Lemonade Lucy."

Hayes did face challenges as president. In July 1877, a massive strike by railroad workers halted trains all over the country. Many politicians and railroad executives urged Hayes to put the railroads under federal control, or to use troops to break up the strike. Hayes did send federal troops to keep order in several cities, but he refused to take sides. The president also refused to sign legislation aimed at keeping Chinese immigrants out of the country.

Hayes was a popular president, and he might have won a second term. But Hayes—who called the presidency "this life of bondage, responsibility, and toil"—decided not to seek reelection.

Hayes's last years were busy. The former president worked for a variety of causes, especially the movement for prison reform. On January 7, 1893, he died of a heart attack, aged seventy.

President Hayes (left) samples the shellfish at a Grand Army of the Republic clambake in Rhode Island in this newspaper illustration. (The Grand Army of the Republic was a large and politically powerful organization of Union Civil War veterans.) Hayes also went to California in September 1880, becoming the first president to visit the West Coast while in office.

Railroad workers rioted during a bitter strike in 1877, the first real test of the presidency of Rutherford Hayes. This lithograph (below) depicts the bloody events of July 20, when the 6th Maryland militia opened fire on striking workers, killing twelve.

JAMES GARFIELD: EARLY YEARS

The last president to be born in a log cabin, James Abram Garfield was born in Orange, Ohio, on November 19, 1831. His father died less than two years later, leaving Eliza Ballou Garfield to raise James and his three brothers and sisters on her own.

Young James was too busy helping his family survive to go to school regularly. Instead, he spent his boyhood working as a hired hand on local farms to bring in money. At age sixteen, Garfield became seriously ill—probably with malaria. When he recovered, his mother, a strong believer in education, gave him her entire savings—$17—so he could finally go to school.

Garfield made up for lost time. After attending local schools, he graduated from Williams College in Massachusetts in 1856. Garfield returned to Ohio the following year to begin a four-year stint as a teacher and principal at Hiram Eclectic Institute, later Hiram College. He was also active in the Disciples of Christ church: Religion would always play an important part in Garfield's life. In 1858, Garfield married Lucretia Rudolph, whom he had courted, off and on, since 1849.

Deciding that "teaching is not the work in which a man can live and grow," Garfield turned to politics. In 1859, he won a seat in the Ohio state senate as a Republican.

Lucretia Rudolph Garfield (1832–1913; above), called "Crete" by her husband, was a quiet woman who overcame her natural shyness to help her husband advance his career. The first years of their marriage were a difficult time, as politics and then the Civil War led to long separations between them. In the late 1870s, James confided to his diary that Lucretia was "the light of my life."

As a teacher, Garfield sometimes used his strength to deal with troublemakers, as this cartoon (opposite, top) shows. It depicts an incident that supposedly took place during Garfield's time as principal of Hiram Eclectic Institute. When local bullies cut the ropes holding up a tent in which Garfield was lecturing, the future president picked up two of them and tossed them out by their collars.

This 1882 painting (right) by James Hope shows Garfield's one-room log cabin birthplace in Orange, Ohio. According to the artist, "The boy carrying the stone across the brook represents the future President." Later in life, Garfield became annoyed at people who made much of his impoverished rural childhood. "Let no man praise me because I was poor" he once said. "It was . . . in every way bad for my life."

MILITARY AND POLITICAL CAREER

When the Civil War began in 1861, Garfield helped organize the 42nd Ohio Volunteers, and he became the regiment's commander, holding the rank of lieutenant colonel. Unlike many of the Civil War's politicians-turned-soldiers, Garfield worked and studied to become a good officer. His superiors recognized his abilities, and at thirty he became the youngest brigadier general in the Union Army. Garfield saw action in Kentucky and at the battles of Shiloh and Chickamauga. In September 1863, he was promoted to major general of volunteers.

Garfield was elected to Congress while still on active duty. At the end of 1863, he left the army to take up his seat in the House of Representatives. He remained in the House for the next seventeen years, eventually serving on the influential Appropriations and Ways and Means committees. Garfield was a loyal Republican, but he held moderate views and tried to stay out of the bitter political battles of Reconstruction.

Representative Garfield was involved in one of the major political scandals of the era. He was accused of taking a $329 payment from the Crédit Mobilier, a phony stock company that used bribes to get important railroad legislation passed in Congress. In 1873, an investigating committee found Garfield innocent of any wrongdoing, but the charge of corruption lingered for the rest of his political career.

Like his predecessor Rutherford Hayes, Garfield (shown here in uniform, above) was proud of his Civil War service. Garfield was reluctant to leave the army after he got the news of his election to the House of Representatives in 1862. It took a personal appeal from President Lincoln to persuade him to resign his officer's commission and come to Washington in December 1863.

This lithograph (opposite, top) shows the Garfield family about the time of James Garfield's election to the presidency. At far left is the president's eldest son, James Rudolph Garfield (1865–1950), who later served as secretary of the interior in Theodore Roosevelt's cabinet.

During the bloody battle of Chickamauga (part of which is depicted in this sketch by A. R. Waud, right) in September 1863, Garfield, then serving on the staff of General William Rosecrans, braved heavy Confederate fire to deliver an important message. His bravery won him promotion to major general.

GARFIELD TAKES OFFICE

In 1880, Garfield was elected to the Senate to replace Senator John Sherman, who stepped down to make a bid for the 1880 Republican presidential nomination. Garfield also agreed to run Sherman's presidential campaign.

There was little support for Sherman at the Republican Convention, however. The party was split into two groups: the "Stalwarts," who wanted former President Ulysses S. Grant to return to the White House, and the "Half-Breeds," who favored Senator James G. Blaine of Maine. With the party divided, no candidate received enough votes for the nomination. Finally, after thirty-five ballots, the convention nominated James Garfield. A moderate with a good war record and an excellent speaker, Garfield seemed like the ideal compromise candidate. Chester Arthur of New York, a Stalwart, got the vice presidential nomination.

Facing Garfield was Democratic candidate Winfield Scott Hancock, a Civil War hero with little political experience. Garfield received a majority of less than 10,000 in the popular vote, although he won a solid majority in the Electoral College.

The president-elect looked on his victory not with enthusiasm but with worry. "I know I am bidding good-bye to my old freedom," he wrote after the election. "I know many will be disappointed with me."

Winfield Scott Hancock (1824–86; above) was one of the Union Army's best generals. He had little political experience, however. The Republicans attacked him by distributing thousands of copies of a pamphlet titled "A Record of the Statesmanship and Political Achievements of General Winfield Scott Hancock, Compiled from the Records." All its pages were blank.

Garfield kept a diary for much of his adult life. This page (right), written on November 3 and 4, 1880, records his thoughts after receiving the news of his election. Telegrams of congratulation had poured into the Garfields' Ohio home. Four months later, after his inauguration, Garfield ended the entry for March 4 with the words "very weary."

A Republican campaign poster (right) shows "Farmer Garfield" cutting his way to the White House through a field choked with the weeds and snakes of fraud and corruption. Garfield fends them off by wielding the scythe of "honesty, ability, and patriotism."

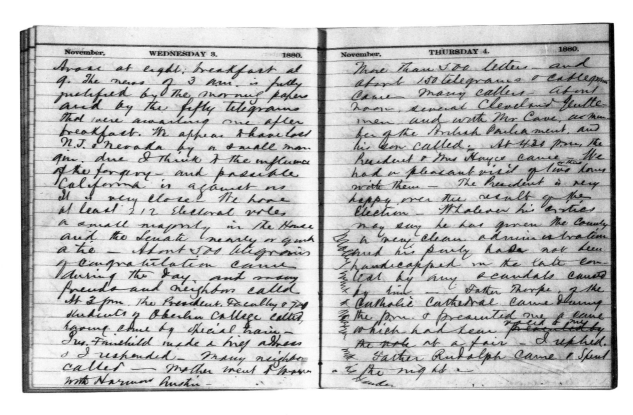

THE ASSASSINATION OF GARFIELD

Garfield's worries turned out to be justified. In the two months following his inauguration, the new president worked to heal the split within the Republican Party. Then, in May, Lucretia Garfield fell ill with malaria. She recovered by the summer of 1881, but anxiety over her health, plus the strain of the presidency, took its toll on Garfield's own health. Garfield decided that he and Lucretia should vacation on the New Jersey shore to escape the heat of a Washington summer.

In early July, Garfield returned to Washington briefly before beginning a tour of New England. The president arrived at Washington's Baltimore & Potomac Railroad Station shortly after 9:00 a.m. on July 2. Charles J. Guiteau, an unstable man who had unsuccessfully sought a diplomatic post in the Garfield administration, was waiting for him. Guiteau drew a pistol and shot the president twice. Garfield crumpled to the floor of the station, badly wounded.

The president was carried to the White House, where he lay in great pain for five weeks. In September, doctors moved Garfield to the New Jersey shore, hoping the sea air and cooler temperatures would help him recover. But on September 19, James Garfield, the second president felled by an assassin's bullet, died at the age of forty-nine. His presidency had lasted just two hundred days.

This lithograph shows the shooting of President Garfield in the Baltimore & Potomac Railroad Station. As Garfield talked with Secretary of State William Evarts, the assassin, Charles J. Guiteau, fired two shots at the president. Tearing at his coat, Garfield cried out, "Oh, my God! What is that?" before falling to the station floor. Nearby policemen quickly grabbed Guiteau.

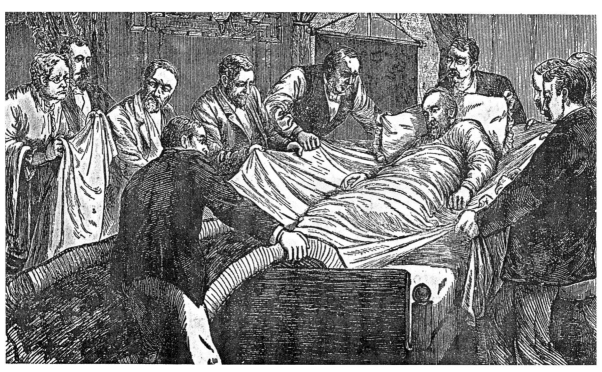

Charles J. Guiteau (c. 1840–82; left) showed up at the White House and the State Department several times in the spring of 1881, seeking an appointment as U.S. consul to Paris. Repeatedly turned down and finally turned away, Guiteau, a lawyer and member of the unpopular Stalwart Party, decided to kill the president.

An ailing President Garfield (below) is moved from the blistering summer heat of Washington, D.C. to the seashore at Elberon, New Jersey. It was hoped that the more mild climate would hasten the president's full recovery. Garfield lingered at Elberon until his death on September 19, 1881.

A handcuffed Guiteau arrives for his murder trial on November 14, 1881, in this engraving (right). Garfield died from blood poisoning, rather than the wound inflicted by Guiteau. Some historians have argued that it was poor medical care, rather than Guiteau's bullet, that actually killed the president.

Guiteau proved an entertaining defendant, given to comic outbursts that sometimes had the jury in stitches, as shown in this cartoon (below). Some spectators believed that Guiteau's amusement at his ordeal was proof of insanity. Guiteau was found guilty on January 25, 1882. He was hanged at Washington's city jail five months later.

CHESTER ARTHUR: EARLY YEARS

Chester Alan Arthur was born in North Fairfield, Vermont, on October 5, 1830. Many years later, Arthur's political enemies claimed that he had actually been born across the border in Canada, which would have disqualified him from serving as president. There is no evidence to support this claim, however.

Arthur's father, a traveling Baptist minister, moved from church to church, so Chester lived in several Vermont and upstate New York towns as a boy. After attending public schools, Arthur worked as a teacher in Pownal, Vermont, to earn money for his education.

Arthur entered Union College in Schenectady, New York, graduating in 1848. He returned to Pownal and resumed his teaching job but, like James Garfield, decided he wasn't cut out for a career in education. He began studying law, and in 1854 Arthur moved to New York City to open a law practice. Arthur also became involved in politics, first as a member of the Whig Party and then as a Republican. In October 1859, Arthur married twenty-two-year-old Ellen Herndon, the Virginia-born daughter of a naval officer.

In 1860, Arthur became engineer in chief on the military staff of New York governor Edwin Morgan. The job was mostly ceremonial in peacetime, but the coming of the Civil War in 1861 gave it new importance.

Ellen Herndon Arthur (1837–80; above), called "Nell," came from a Southern family. During the Civil War, Chester Arthur liked to call her "my little Rebel wife." When Arthur traveled to war-torn Virginia on an inspection trip in 1862, he visited his wife's relatives, including an uncle, who wrote that Arthur "was very affectionate and kind."

This print (right) shows how Broadway in New York City looked in 1855, the year after Arthur arrived in the city to begin his law practice. In one of his first cases, Arthur successfully sued a streetcar company on behalf of a black woman who had been barred from one of the company's vehicles because of her race. The case brought the young lawyer to the attention of the city's newly formed Republican Party.

Chester Arthur (right) was a sharp dresser—he ordered his suits from London's best tailors—who took great care with his appearance. He was especially proud of his beard. Worn in the "mutton-chop" style of the day, his whiskers were always trimmed to perfection. As a powerful figure in New York City's Republican circles, Arthur was known as the "Gentleman Boss" for his luxurious life-style.

ARTHUR: POLITICAL BOSS

At the outbreak of the Civil War, the federal government was too small to organize the tens of thousands of men who volunteered to fight for the Union. The state governments had to take on the job. Chester Arthur was quickly promoted to quartermaster general, responsible for keeping New York's volunteer troops fed and supplied. He did a good job, but when Governor Morgan failed to win reelection in 1862, Arthur lost his post.

Arthur spent the next eight years practicing law and working as a party manager for New York's Republicans. In 1871, President Ulysses S. Grant appointed Arthur Collector of the Port of New York, an important civil service position that put him in charge of more than 1,000 employees.

The appointment made Arthur a controversial figure. The 1870s were a time when government corruption was common, especially in the Civil Service. Many Civil Service appointees seemed more interested in using their jobs to get rich than in serving the public. Arthur was accused of allowing his employees to profit illegally from their positions. Arthur himself was said to have gained $40,000 by using his influence to get political allies jobs in the Civil Service.

In 1878, vowing to end corruption in the Civil Service, President Rutherford Hayes fired Arthur. Personal tragedy followed this political setback. In 1880, Ellen Arthur died of pneumonia.

Ellen and Chester Arthur had three children. A son, William Lewis Herndon Arthur, was born in 1863 but died before his third birthday. Chester Alan Arthur, Jr. (1864–1937) and Ellen Herndon Arthur (1871–1915) lived to adulthood. This photograph (left) shows how Ellen Arthur looked when her father was president. Her mother did not live to see Chester Arthur become president. Arthur brought her portrait to the White House and put fresh flowers in front of it every day.

Titled "The Kings of Wall Street," this print (below) shows some of New York's most powerful businessmen of the 1860s and 1870s, including Jay Gould and Commodore William Vanderbilt, who sit opposite each other at the center table. After the Civil War, business and politics mixed closely in New York. Politicians like Chester Arthur were usually willing to support laws that favored big business—in return for financial favors.

CHESTER ARTHUR TAKES OFFICE

Despite the controversy over his years as Collector of the Port of New York, Arthur remained a powerful figure in the Republican Party, especially among the "Stalwart" group led by New York Senator Roscoe Conkling. At the Republican Convention in 1880, Arthur was nominated as James Garfield's running mate to win Stalwart support for the ticket. Conkling urged Arthur to refuse the nomination, but Arthur accepted.

Just four months after taking office, Garfield was shot and seriously wounded. In the eighty days between Garfield's shooting and his death, Vice President Arthur kept a low profile, although Garfield was too badly hurt to perform his duties as president. But when Garfield died on September 19, 1881, Arthur had to face facts: He was now the nation's twenty-first president.

"Chet Arthur President of the United States! Good God!" said one leading Republican when he heard the news of Garfield's death. Many Americans shared this feeling of shock. Arthur had never held an elected office before winning the vice presidency. Most Americans identified him with the corruption of the 1870s. And in contrast with presidents Hayes and Garfield— both of them modest, religious men— Arthur was well known for his flashy clothes and love of luxurious living.

The cover of Frank Leslie's Illustrated Newspaper (right) shows Chester Arthur registering to vote in New York City in October 1882. By this time, Arthur's commitment to honest government and civil service reform had frustrated many of his former political friends in New York. "He ain't Chet Arthur anymore" one of them reportedly said. "He's the President."

This political cartoon (below) depicts a crowd of corrupt politicians protesting President Arthur's efforts to make the Civil Service more honest and efficient. The legislature responded to Arthur's pledge by forming a five-man commission to oversee the Civil Service, and in 1883 it sent the Pendleton Civil Service Act to Arthur, who signed it into law.

FRANK LESLIE'S
ILLUSTRATED
NEWSPAPER

Entered according to Act of Congress, in the year 1862, by Mrs. FRANK LESLIE, in the Office of the Librarian of Congress at Washington.— Entered at the Post Office, New York, N.Y., as Second-class Matter.

No. 1,414.—Vol. LV.]   NEW YORK—FOR THE WEEK ENDING OCTOBER 28, 1882.   [PRICE 10 CENTS.

NEW YORK CITY.—PRESIDENT ARTHUR REGISTERING AS A VOTER AT THE REGISTRATION OFFICE, No. 402 THIRD AVENUE.

FROM A SKETCH BY A STAFF ARTIST.—SEE PAGE 151.

CHESTER ARTHUR: LATER YEARS

Arthur's commitment to end political corruption surprised many people. He was not afraid to veto politically popular bills, including the Rivers and Harbors Act of 1882, that would have served mostly to put money in politicians' pockets.

As president, Chester Arthur changed his political style when he became president, but not his personal style. As a widower, Arthur had no First Lady, but his sister Mary Arthur McElroy served as White House hostess. Arthur loved to entertain, and the White House was often the scene of lively parties where choice food and wine flowed freely. "I may be President of the United States," he said to a woman who criticized his lavish lifestyle, "but my private life is nobody's damned business."

Although Arthur proved to be a much better president than most Americans expected, his policies angered many Republicans, and he wasn't renominated in 1884. Arthur suffered from health problems during his presidency, and he died in New York City on November 18, 1886, less than two years after leaving office. He was fifty-six years old.

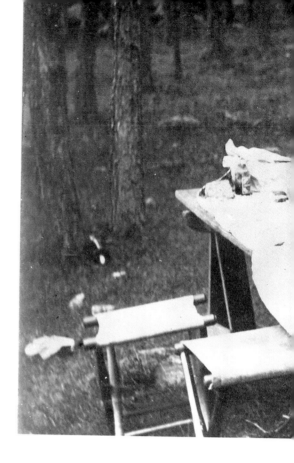

In this photograph (above), Arthur and a friend relax during an 1882 camping trip along the St. Lawrence River in upstate New York. Arthur was not one of the hardest-working presidents. His lack of energy came, at least in part, from poor health. As president, he suffered from Bright's Disease, a serious kidney ailment. Realizing he might not live through a second term, Arthur did not press for his party's renomination.

Arthur's accomplishments as president were a pleasant surprise to many Americans, but others felt he didn't do enough. This cartoon (right) from the humorous magazine Judge shows Santa Claus bringing gifts to the president, including a "new backbone."

GROVER CLEVELAND: EARLY YEARS

The son of a Presbyterian minister, Stephen Grover Cleveland was born on March 18, 1837, in Caldwell, New Jersey. The family moved to western New York State when Grover was a young child.

In 1853, Grover's father died. Responsibility for supporting the family fell on Grover, who had to quit school and begin working to provide for his mother and eight brothers and sisters. After working for a year in a school for the blind in New York City, he decided to try his luck on the frontier. He got no farther west than Buffalo, New York, where a prosperous uncle offered to help him study law. Cleveland accepted and began practicing in Buffalo in 1859. Soon involved in local politics as a Democrat, he became assistant district attorney of Erie County in 1863.

Later that year Cleveland was drafted to serve in the Union Army. During the Civil War, drafted men could hire substitutes to enter the army in their places, and this is what Cleveland did. He had a good reason for staying out of the army—his mother and unmarried sisters depended on his financial support. Later, however, he would be called a draft dodger and coward.

After an unsuccessful run for district attorney in 1865, Cleveland left politics to concentrate on his law practice.

Cleveland came to the White House a bachelor. He enlisted the help of his younger sister, Rose Elizabeth Cleveland (above), to pitch in as Washington's premier hostess. Rose retired from her duties when Cleveland married twenty-one-year-old Frances Folsom, the youngest bride ever to become First Lady.

Although Cleveland had strong personal and political roots in Buffalo, he was born in this quiet country home (opposite, top) in Caldwell, New Jersey. Cleveland moved to Buffalo when he was sixteen years old, following the death of his father.

This engraving (right) shows Buffalo's Main Street in the mid-nineteenth century. Buffalo was a booming city when Grover Cleveland arrived in 1855, thanks to its location at the western end of the Erie Canal, which connected the port of New York City with the Great Lakes.

CLEVELAND THE REFORMER

Apart from a single term (1871–73) as sheriff of Erie County, Cleveland remained a private citizen until 1882. The heavyset lawyer enjoyed a bachelor's life in Buffalo, spending his Sunday afternoons drinking beer and playing poker with his friends.

In 1881, Cleveland was elected mayor of Buffalo. It was the beginning of a swift three-year rise to the White House. "Being mayor of Buffalo never would have made Cleveland famous," one historian has written, "but being an honest mayor of any city of the United States at that time . . . was a distinction unfortunately rare." Cleveland was soon famous throughout New York State for his successful reform of Buffalo's corrupt city government. Frustrated local politicians nicknamed Cleveland the "veto mayor" for his refusal to sign bills aimed at enriching them at the public's expense.

The state's Democratic organization, eager to use Cleveland's growing reputation to their advantage, nominated him for governor in 1882. With the support of reform-minded Republicans as well as Democrats, Cleveland was easily elected. As governor, he continued his drive for honest government at the state level. Soon his reputation spread beyond New York. With the election of 1884 approaching, Democratic leaders began to see Cleveland as the one candidate who could end the Republican Party's long hold on the White House.

Cleveland and Reform.

GOV. GROVER CLEVELAND.

22ND. PRESIDENT OF THE UNITED STATES.

This unusual campaign poster for Grover Cleveland's 1884 presidential bid (above) is surrounded by quotes that highlight Cleveland's superior qualifications for the office. Some are inspirational, reminding voters of his belief in honest government. Others cite press clippings about a corrupt railroad industry that only a strong, reform minded president, like Cleveland, could address.

Cleveland always tried to do what he considered the right thing, even if it meant losing his popularity with voters. A case in point came during his time as governor of New York, when he vetoed a bill to lower fares on New York City's elevated railroads. This print (right) shows Franklin Square in New York City about the time Cleveland became governor of the state.

HANOVER SQUARE STATION

THE CAMPAIGN OF 1884

At the 1884 Democratic Convention, Cleveland easily won the party's presidential nomination, with Thomas A. Hendricks of Indiana as his running mate. The Republicans nominated Senator James G. Blaine of Maine.

Blaine proved to be a controversial candidate. Already tainted by connection to several scandals of the 1870s, Blaine's candidacy suffered a blow when a Democratic newspaper published letters linking him with a shady business deal. Many anti-Blaine Republicans, dubbed "Mugwumps," switched their support to Cleveland.

But other Republicans dug into Cleveland's past and hit pay dirt. A Buffalo newspaper reported that as a young man, Cleveland had fathered an illegitimate son with a local widow, Maria Halpin. Cleveland decided to face the accusation. He admitted his relationship with the woman (although whether he was actually the father was never proved) and showed that he had supported the child and his mother. The scandal probably cost Cleveland many votes, but his honesty impressed other Americans.

The bitter campaign ended in a very close election. Cleveland received only about 10,000 more popular votes than Blaine, but it was enough to give him a decisive majority in the Electoral College. Grover Cleveland became the first Democrat elected president since James Buchanan in 1856.

"Another voice for Cleveland" is the title of this pro-Republican cartoon (above) from the presidential campaign of 1884. The Republicans made much of Cleveland's illegitimate child as the election approached, but the candidate ordered his campaign managers not to dig up embarrassing facts about James G. Blaine, insisting that "the other side can have a monopoly of all the dirt in this campaign."

A giant crowd in Buffalo celebrates Grover Cleveland's nomination for president in this newspaper illustration (right). At Democratic rallies, Cleveland supporters often chanted "Blaine! Blaine! the continental liar from the state of Maine!" Not to be outdone, Republicans shouted "Ma, Ma, Where's my Pa?" When Cleveland won, however, the Democrats replied—"Gone to the White House! Ha, Ha, Ha!"

CLEVELAND'S FIRST TERM

Cleveland's happy marriage to Frances Folsom was soon followed by a fierce political battle. During the Civil War, Congress had enacted high tariffs—taxes on imported goods—to protect American industries from overseas competition. In the years after the war, the tariffs brought in so much money that the federal treasury had a large surplus. Many congressmen wanted to reduce this surplus by giving aid to farmers and increasing pensions for Civil War veterans. Cleveland, who was conservative on economic issues, vetoed all these measures. In December 1887, the president announced that he wanted the tariffs lowered, and he made tariff reduction the chief issue of his campaign for re-election in 1888.

The Republicans, who supported high tariffs, spent millions of dollars on the campaign of their candidate, Senator Benjamin Harrison of Indiana. In another close election, Cleveland won about 100,000 more popular votes than Harrison, but lost the Electoral College—and the election—to the Republican challenger.

Frances Folsom (1864–1947; above) was the daughter of Oscar Folsom, once a law partner of Cleveland's. After Frances's father died in an accident in 1875, Cleveland acted as guardian for Frances and remained a close friend of the Folsom family. Grover and Frances became engaged in 1885, but they kept the engagement a secret until the spring of 1886.

Hardworking President Cleveland scheduled his White House wedding for the evening of June 2, 1886, so he could put in a full day's work. Cleveland also wrote the wedding invitations himself. Some people were shocked by the wedding ceremony (shown opposite, top) because the couple deliberately cut the command "to obey" from Frances's part of the wedding vows.

Many Americans supported high tariffs on imports so that British goods would be kept off American markets, allowing American industries to grow. President Cleveland, however, favored lower tariffs. This pro-high-tariffs cartoon (right) shows Cleveland taking orders from "John Bull," a figure representing Britain. The crowd behind Cleveland represents unemployed Irish workers, who had resented British rule in Ireland.

Part II
Conflict at Home, Expansion Abroad

In this 1893 illustration, Grover Cleveland pulls a cart carrying Adlai Stevenson, vice president during Cleveland's second term. It portrays the enthusiasm Cleveland inspired among average Americans, who relished his commitment to reform and his stubborn political independence in the face of powerful party bosses. Cleveland is the only president ever to reclaim the White House in a non-consecutive second term.

The 1890s marked the end of one era in American history and the beginning of another. For more than a century, the nation had moved westward, filling up the vast spaces of the continent with people and settlements. As the turn of the century approached, the era of Western expansion came to an end. Now that the United States was settled from coast to coast, many Americans believed it was time for the nation to take its place as a world power. By the end of the century, the United States was indeed a world power, thanks to its victory in the Spanish-American War.

As the nation changed, so did the presidency. Throughout the nineteenth century, foreign policy had been a minor concern for American presidents. From William McKinley's administration on, maintaining America's role in the world would become an increasingly important part of the president's job, although throughout the 1890s, foreign policy still came second to domestic concerns.

In 1893, as Grover Cleveland began his second term, a terrible economic depression set in. Partly as a result of these hard times, a new force—Populism—emerged in American politics. The new Populist Party, supported by its allies in the Democratic Party, called for free circulation of money and other measures to ease the burdens of the nation's farmers and workers. Although Populism was defeated at the polls in 1896 and 1900, many of its goals were achieved by twentieth-century presidents.

BENJAMIN HARRISON: EARLY YEARS

The only grandson of a president to reach the White House himself, Benjamin Harrison was born on August 20, 1833, in North Bend, Ohio. His grandfather was William Henry Harrison, frontier soldier and ninth president of the United States. Comparisons with his famous grandfather always annoyed Benjamin Harrison, who wanted to be respected for his own ability and not his ancestry. "I want it understood that I am the grandson of nobody," he said as a young man. "I believe that every man should stand on his own merits." But considering his family history (his father was also a politician), it seemed only natural that Harrison would pursue a career in law and politics.

While attending Miami University in Oxford, Ohio, Harrison fell in love with Caroline Lavinia Scott, the daughter of a Presbyterian minister. They were married in 1853, a year after Harrison's graduation. Harrison was admitted to the bar the same year. In 1854, the Harrisons moved to Indianapolis, Indiana, where Benjamin set up a law practice. It took several years for Harrison to prosper, but by the late 1850s he was one of the most prominent attorneys in the city.

Harrison also became involved in the activities of the newly formed Republican Party. His political career began in 1857 with his election as Indianapolis city attorney.

This photograph (above) of Caroline Scott Harrison (1832–92) was taken in 1889, at the beginning of Benjamin Harrison's presidency. The two met when Benjamin was a student at Farmer's College, where Caroline's minister father taught math and science. A graduate of Ohio's Oxford Female Institute, Caroline worked as a music teacher until her marriage to Harrison in October 1853.

This print (opposite, top) shows Benjamin Harrison's birthplace—a farm in North Bend, Ohio, five miles down the Ohio River from the mansion built by his grandfather William Harrison. Because the farm was far from town, John Harrison built a one-room schoolhouse on his own property and hired teachers to instruct Benjamin and his eight brothers and sisters.

At age fourteen, Benjamin Harrison went away to Farmer's College, a private school near Cincinnati, to prepare for college. The paper shown here (right), taken from his school notes, is young Harrison's summary of a book on "mental philosophy." Harrison's keen mind and precise way of thinking would later make him one of the nation's most effective lawyers and a capable politician.

Philosophy

Part II Sensibilities	Part III	Part IIII
Natural or Pathematic sensibil.	Moral sensibilities or conscience	Disorders sensitive action
ch. Introduction	Classifications of the Sensibilities	
Class I Emotions	ch. Content of Chapters	1st disorders action
1 Nature of the Emotion	1st Emotions of moral approbation	of the Appe. proper
2 Emotions of Beauty	2 Relations of reasoning to... nature...	2d Sympathetic imita...
3 Associated Beauty	3 Feelings of moral obligation	3d disorders action
4 Emotions of Sublimity	4 Uniformity of action in men see	of the Affection
5 Emotion of the Ludicrous	5th Moral Education	4th disorders action
6 Instances of other simp. Em.	Definition &c	of the moral sensibilit...
Class II Desire		Miscellaneous
1 Nature of desire		
2 Instincts		
3 Appetites		
4 Propensities		
5 Malevolent Affections		
6 Benevolent Affections		
7 Love to the supreme being		
8 Habits of the sensibilities		
Definition		

HARRISON: ABILITY, ENERGY, AND GALLANTRY

With the coming of the Civil War, Harrison joined the Union Army. On July 14, 1862, he became a second lieutenant in the Indiana Volunteers. A short time later he was promoted to captain and given command of a company in the 70th Indiana Regiment, a unit that he had helped organize at the request of Indiana governor Oliver P. Morton. Harrison remained with the 70th Indiana through most of the war, eventually rising to colonel and commander of the regiment.

Harrison took part in General William Tecumseh Sherman's campaign to capture the important Confederate city of Atlanta, Georgia, but his services to the Union went beyond the battlefield. After the fall of Atlanta in September 1864, Harrison returned to Indiana to recruit new volunteers. He also worked against the state's "Copperheads"—Northerners who supported the Confederacy. Harrison finally left the army in June 1865 with the rank of brigadier general.

With the war over, Harrison returned to his law practice. In 1876, he lost a close race for the governorship of Indiana. Many of his supporters believed he lost the election not because of his policies, but because of his personality. Harrison had a keen mind and was a brilliant speaker, but he came across as aloof and distant in face-to-face campaigning. One person described him as a "human iceberg."

Harrison, shown here (right) in his army uniform astride his horse, spent his Civil War career with the 70th Indiana Regiment. Harrison personally recruited and organized the 70th Indiana. Besides active military service, Harrison managed to serve as reporter of Indiana's state Supreme Court in 1864.

In this engraving (below), Union forces storm one of the Confederate fortifications protecting Atlanta. Colonel Benjamin Harrison saw plenty of combat in the campaign to capture the city during the summer and fall of 1864. For his ability and bravery, Harrison's superiors recommended him for an honorary promotion to brigadier general.

HARRISON WINS THE WHITE HOUSE

In 1888, after only one term in the Senate and a failed bid for reelection, Harrison emerged as the leading candidate for the Republican presidential nomination. At the Republican Convention in Chicago, Harrison won the nomination on the eighth ballot. Levi Morton, a New York businessman, got the vice presidential nomination.

Harrison didn't campaign actively. Instead, he stayed at home in Indianapolis, giving speeches to groups of visitors. But the Republicans were better organized and financed than the Democrats, and Harrison won a majority in the Electoral College, although incumbent Democrat Grover Cleveland received more popular votes.

In the White House, Harrison made good on his promise to support high tariffs; the McKinley Tariff Act, passed by Congress in 1890, raised tariffs to the highest level ever. He also supported two other major pieces of economic legislation: the Sherman Anti-Trust Act, which broke up business monopolies, and the Sherman Silver Purchase Act, which called for increased coinage of silver. This would raise the amount of money in circulation, allowing farmers and small business people to pay off debts more easily.

Levi P. Morton (1824–1920; above), Benjamin Harrison's running mate in 1888, was a wealthy New York City banker who contributed much of his fortune to the Republican Party. Despite limited political experience, he proved to be a capable and respected vice president, and he later won election to the governorship of New York.

This 1889 photograph (opposite, top) shows four generations of the Harrison family gathered at the White House; from left to right, Caroline Harrison, holding her grandson, two-year-old Benjamin Harrison McKee; Mary Harrison McKee (1858–1930), daughter of Benjamin and Caroline Harrison; and baby Mary L. McKee, in the lap of Reverend John Witherspoon Scott, Caroline Harrison's father.

Republican campaign literature from the election of 1888—including this sheet music cover (right)—made much of Harrison's connection to his grandfather, President William Henry Harrison. ("Grandfather's Hat Fits Ben!" was one campaign slogan.)

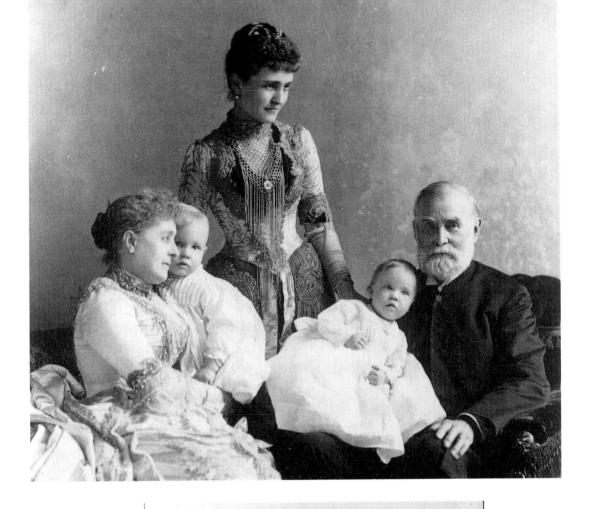

BENJAMIN HARRISON: LATER YEARS

Benjamin Harrison's presidency marked the beginning of a change in American foreign policy. Many American business people and politicians—including President Harrison—now believed the nation should take a more active role in international affairs. Thus, Harrison supported a naval buildup, sponsored a conference of Latin American nations in 1889, and tried (unsuccessfully) to annex Hawaii to the United States when a revolution overthrew the islands' native monarchy.

The Republicans nominated Harrison for reelection in 1892, although the president had angered many party members by refusing to grant jobs and favors to political allies. The Democrats once again nominated Grover Cleveland.

On October 25, 1892, Caroline Harrison died of tuberculosis. Two weeks later, Harrison received another blow; Cleveland easily recaptured the White House. Compared to the loss of his wife, Harrison said, the defeat at the polls "had no sting in it."

Harrison left office and began an active retirement. In 1896, he remarried, to his wife's niece, Mary Scott Dimmick. Besides maintaining his law practice, Harrison lectured at Stanford University and authored three books. On March 31, 1901, Benjamin Harrison died of pneumonia at home in Indianapolis, aged sixty-seven.

After leaving the White House, newly widowed Benjamin Harrison returned to this house (right) in Indianapolis, where he died in 1901. Learning of Harrison's death, then-president William McKinley said, "The country has been deprived of one of its greatest citizens. A brilliant soldier . . . an orator and legislator . . . he displayed extraordinary gifts as an administrator and statesman. In public and private life he set a shining example."

Political cartoonists liked to make fun of Harrison's height (he was only about five-feet-six-inches tall). The artist of this 1892 cartoon (below) believed Harrison was too small to wear his grandfather's hat. Other people found fault with the president's handshake—"like a wilted petunia," said one acquaintance.

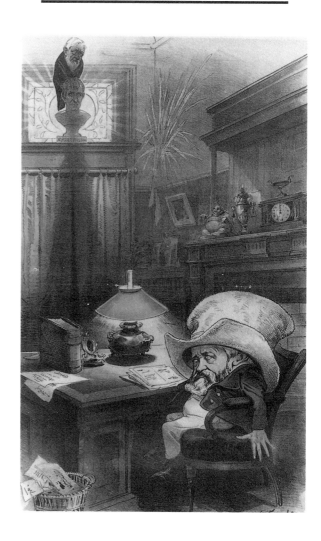

In April 1896, the widowed ex-president remarried, to Mary Scott Dimmick (1858–1948; right). Harrison's children opposed the marriage: Besides being Caroline Harrison's niece, Mary Dimmick was twenty-five years younger than Benjamin. The couple had one child, Elizabeth Harrison, who was younger than Harrison's four grandchildren.

CLEVELAND'S COMEBACK

On the day Grover and Frances Cleveland left the White House in 1889, the First Lady told the White House doorman that they would be back "just four years from today." Her prediction turned out to be true; in 1892, Grover Cleveland became the only former president reelected to a second, non-consecutive term.

After the end of his first term, Cleveland settled in New York City, becoming a partner in one of the city's foremost law firms. Many Democrats still disliked Cleveland for his stubborn refusal to follow the party line when it conflicted with his own beliefs. Others, however, saw him as the one Democrat who could regain the White House in 1892. At the party's Chicago convention, Cleveland was nominated for another term on the first ballot.

Cleveland faced the same opponent as in 1888: Benjamin Harrison. But both Cleveland and Harrison were challenged by a new third party: the Populists, or "People's Party." Strongest in the farming states of the West and the South, the Populists favored major economic reforms, including an income tax and increased silver coinage, to improve conditions for farmers and industrial workers. The party's candidate, James B. Weaver, won over a million popular votes. Cleveland overcame both Harrison and the Populist challenge, winning solid majorities in both the popular vote and the Electoral College.

In 1892, the Republicans circulated this poster (opposite, top), which pictures Cleveland against a map of the United States. The map shows what the Republicans believed would happen if Cleveland were reelected—the mines and factories of the northern states would face "destruction." The poster also implies that Cleveland would only admit Western territories to the Union if they had mostly Democratic voting populations.

Uncle Sam in a snappy admiral's uniform greets Grover Cleveland as he comes up the gangplank of the "ship of state" in this 1893 cartoon (right) by G. Y. Coffin. Cleveland carries a bag labeled "Repeal and Reform." The "Repeal" probably refers to the Sherman Silver Purchase Act; many politicians and business people considered the act bad for the economy and hoped to see it repealed.

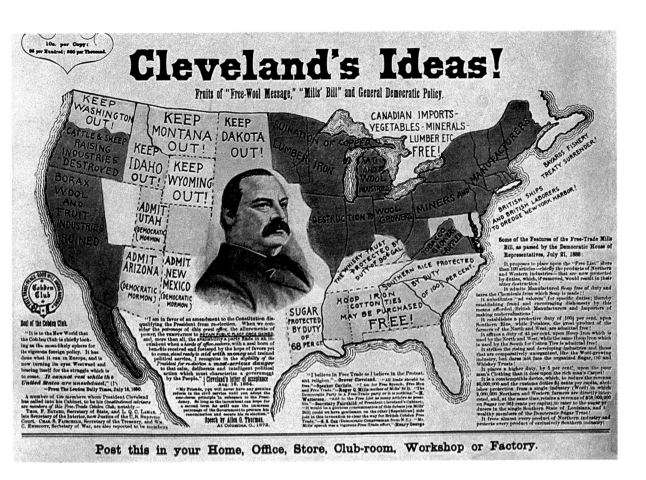

CLEVELAND'S SECOND TERM

Even before he took office, Grover Cleveland's second administration suffered a bad blow. In February 1893, the Philadelphia & Reading Railroad went bankrupt, and four more major railroads followed. This touched off a financial "panic" that soon turned into the worst economic depression in decades. By the end of Cleveland's first year in office, more than 4 million Americans were out of work.

A growing financial crisis added to Cleveland's problems. The Sherman Silver Purchase Act, passed in 1890, required the federal government to purchase silver as well as gold for the federal treasury, and citizens could exchange paper currency for either silver or gold. As the depression worsened, many Americans converted their paper money into gold, which was more valuable than silver. This led to a steep drop in the amount of gold in the federal treasury, which in turn caused the U.S. dollar to lose value.

Cleveland, a "hard-money man," believed that the bad times would end if the country made gold alone the standard for U.S. currency. To accomplish this, he launched a determined effort to get Congress to repeal the Silver Purchase Act. The president won this battle after a special session of Congress repealed the act in November 1893, but the repeal campaign lost Cleveland the support of the many Democrats who supported the Populist demand for more coinage of silver.

Frances Cleveland, shown here (right) in 1897, remained a popular First Lady even as her husband's popularity slipped. She was so popular, in fact, that manufacturers of cosmetics and other products used her name and picture in advertisements—without the First Lady's approval or permission. "Frank," as her husband called her, was a gracious hostess who kept the social side of White House life running smoothly.

For a half-century, Native Americans had been moved, often forcibly, from their homelands and put on reservations in the Indian Territory (now the state of Oklahoma). Starting in the 1880s, the federal government opened the territory to white settlement. Eager to stake their claims, more than 100,000 people rushed into the "Cherokee Strip" on September 16, 1893, as shown in this print (below).

The Pullman strike was the severest test of Cleveland's second
term. In this newspaper illustration (above), Illinois National
Guardsmen fire into a group of striking railroad workers in
Chicago. Federal troops joined the guardsmen after July 3, 1894,
when Cleveland ordered the army to restore order in Chicago and
keep mail trains moving.

The cover of the September 1893 issue of Puck (opposite, top) celebrates the repeal of the Sherman Silver Purchase Act by showing
Uncle Sam and a woman representing the nation's business interests climbing "out of the Silver Flood." Cleveland sought the support of Republican senators to win repeal.

Cleveland and his family spent several summers at this house,
Gray Gables (right), on Buzzards Bay in Massachusetts.

VOL. XXXIV.—No. 852.   PUCK BUILDING, New York, September 13th, 1893.   PRICE, 10 CENTS.

Copyright, 1893, by Keppler & Schwarzmann.

Entered at N. Y. P. O. as Second-class Mail Matter.

Puck

OUT OF THE SILVER FLOOD!

GROVER CLEVELAND: LATER YEARS

During the fight over the Silver Purchase Act, Cleveland learned he was suffering from cancer of the mouth. Fearing the news would alarm an already tense nation, the president kept his condition secret. In July 1893, doctors twice operated on Cleveland aboard a yacht off New York City. Although much of his jaw was removed and replaced with a rubber fitting, Cleveland made a quick recovery.

In the summer of 1894, railroad workers halted trains around the country to support a strike by workers at the Pullman railroad car factory near Chicago. The strike stopped mail service, and Cleveland decided to intervene. In the first use of presidential power to halt a labor dispute, Cleveland issued an order to end the strike, and placed federal troops to Chicago to keep the peace.

By the election year of 1896, Cleveland was unpopular with both the American people and Democratic Party leaders. At the party's 1896 convention, the delegates ignored Cleveland and nominated William Jennings Bryan. The Clevelands retired to Princeton, New Jersey. Cleveland later became a trustee of nearby Princeton University. On June 24, 1908, Cleveland died at the age of seventy-one.

This photograph (right) shows the former president and First Lady with their four children on the steps of the Clevelands' home in Princeton, New Jersey. The Clevelands' first child, Ruth (far left) died in 1904 at the age of twelve. (The Baby Ruth candy bar would be named in her honor.) Her death cast a shadow over the former president's last years.

This cartoon (below), published just before the election of 1896, depicts Cleveland as a fool whose policies have wrecked the economy. The cartoonist measures Cleveland against earlier presidents from Washington to Benjamin Harrison on a sliding scale, implying that the nation's presidents had become increasingly less capable.

WILLIAM McKINLEY: EARLY YEARS

William McKinley was born in Niles, Ohio, on January 29, 1843, the seventh child of William McKinley, Sr., an ironworker, and his wife, Nancy Campbell McKinley. William spent his boyhood in rural Ohio, going to local schools and briefly attending Allegheny College. When his father's business began to decline in the late 1850s, William had to cut short his education and go to work as a schoolteacher in Poland, Ohio.

McKinley joined the Union Army two months after the onset of the Civil War, enlisting as a private in the 23rd Ohio Volunteer Infantry. (The regiment's commander was another future president, Rutherford Hayes.) McKinley was an able soldier, and he quickly moved up through the ranks. By the spring of 1862, he was a sergeant; in September, he was promoted to second lieutenant. Toward the end of the war he fought in the campaign to drive Confederate forces out of Virginia's Shenandoah Valley, winning a temporary promotion to major for his "gallant and meritorious services." He left the army in July 1865. The suffering and death of the Civil War made a deep impression on McKinley. "I have seen war," he said, when, as president, many Americans urged him to declare war on Spain. "I have seen the dead piled up, and I do not want to see another."

This storefront (right) shows the birthplace of William McKinley in Niles, Ohio. The house was sold to a shopkeeper before being torn down. The city of Niles has since erected the National McKinley Birthplace Memorial, which houses memorabilia from McKinley's life and presidency.

In the fall of 1864, McKinley, now a captain, took part in the Battle of Opequon Creek in the Shenandoah Valley—part of which is shown in this painting (below). His commanding officer, Rutherford Hayes, described him "as one of the bravest and finest officers in the army."

McKINLEY: FROM SOLDIER TO GOVERNOR

Returning to Ohio after the war, McKinley decided to study law, and by 1867 he had his own practice in Canton, Ohio. Two years later, he became prosecuting attorney of Stark County.

In 1870, McKinley fell in love with twenty-two-year-old Ida Saxton, the daughter of a local banker, and they were married on January 1, 1871. William and Ida were devoted to each other and shared deep religious convictions—which helped their marriage endure several tragedies. Their first child, Katie, died of typhoid fever at the age of three. Another daughter, Ida, born in 1873, lived only five months. The birth of her second child ruined Ida McKinley's health. For the rest of her life, she suffered from a form of epilepsy. McKinley's tender care for his wife impressed everyone who met the couple. "There is nothing more beautiful," a journalist later wrote, "than his [McKinley's] long devotion to his invalid wife . . ."

In 1876, McKinley was elected to Congress as a Republican, beginning a fourteen-year stint in the House of Representatives. McKinley made himself an expert on the tariff issue, and in 1890 he sponsored the tariff bill that bore his name. Although he failed to win reelection in 1890, McKinley was elected to the first of two terms as governor of Ohio later that year.

Ida Saxton McKinley (1847–1907; left) was working in her father's bank when she first met William McKinley; he was soon bringing her flowers every time he made a deposit. Ida was a witty and energetic young woman, but she was forced to live almost as an invalid after she began experiencing seizures in 1873. Despite her epilepsy and other health problems, she lived for six years after her devoted husband's death.

During McKinley's years in the House, the Ohio representative became an ally of House Speaker Thomas Brackett Reed of Maine. Because some representatives misused Congress's rules to block action on bills, Reed drafted a new set of rules and got them adopted. This 1890 cartoon (below) shows Reed "bowling over" Democrats opposed to the new rules, while McKinley stands behind them, clad in a casual white vest, awaiting the outcome.

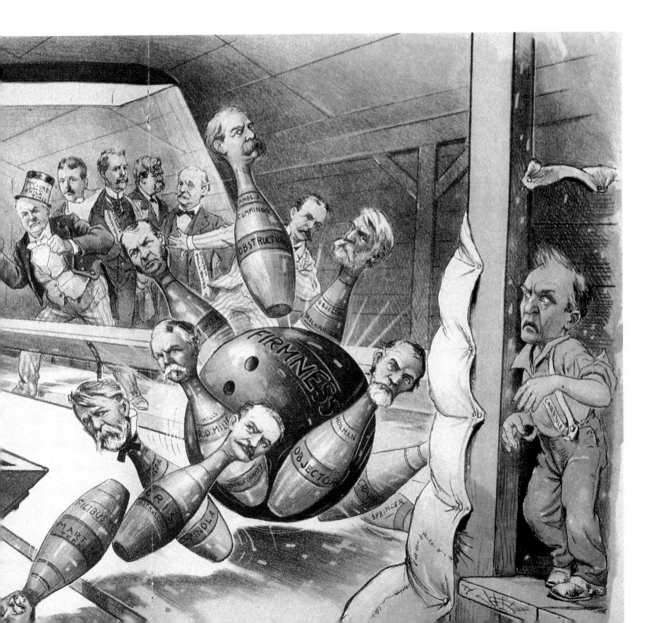

THE ELECTION OF 1896: SILVER V. GOLD

During his years as congressman and governor, McKinley became a close friend of millionaire Mark Hanna. Along with other business leaders and Republican politicians, Hanna promoted McKinley for the presidency in 1896. With Hanna's support—and money—behind him, McKinley easily won the nomination at the Republican's St. Louis convention.

At the Democratic Convention in Chicago, the party turned away from incumbent Grover Cleveland and toward its rising star—William Jennings Bryan.

Born on March 19, 1860, in Illinois, Bryan moved to Nebraska after graduating from Illinois College and studying law in Chicago. Elected to the House in 1890, he soon became one of the Democratic Party's most eloquent champions of free—unlimited—silver coinage. On June 11, Bryan made an impassioned plea against the gold standard and for silver coinage, ending with the phrase "You shall not crucify mankind upon a cross of gold." Bryan wasn't originally considered a possible candidate, but the speech won over the delegates.

While the gold standard versus free silver issue was prominent in the election, the issue had other, more complex meanings. The election pitted Bryan, self-proclaimed champion of the "common man," against McKinley, who had the support of the nation's major industrial leaders.

Although William Jennings Bryan (1860–1925; left) failed to win the presidency in three elections—1896, 1900 and 1908—he served as Woodrow Wilson's secretary of state from 1913 to 1915. He resigned this post, however, because he believed Wilson's foreign policy would lead the United States into war.

A cartoon from Judge (below) depicts Bryan as a fool leading the Democratic Party to disaster. Bryan carries a ball labeled "16 to 1" on his shoulder. This refers to the Democratic and Populist demand that the federal treasury coin silver at a ratio of 16 silver to 1 gold. Bryan's speech at the 1896 Democratic Convention, one of the most famous speeches in American history, was a stirring protest against the gold standard.

THE CAMPAIGN OF 1896

While Bryan campaigned vigorously across the country, McKinley stayed home in Ohio, leaving a highly-organized and well-financed campaign team to push his candidacy. The Republicans made sure McKinley got extensive press coverage, and they sent out as many as five million pieces of pro-McKinley literature a week. The Republican campaign fund was $7 million; Bryan and his supporters could spend only $300,000.

"A war of the East against the West," was how one historian described the election of 1896, "the farmers against the railroad tycoons and bankers; the workers against the industrialists; gold against silver . . ."

It was a war McKinley won. Despite the rapid growth of Populism in much of the country, the heavily populated industrial states of the Northeast and Midwest cast most of their votes for McKinley. (Some factory workers voted for McKinley because their bosses, armed with Republican campaign literature, told them that Bryan's election would lead to economic disaster.) In many ways, the election of 1896 marked a major change in American history: the switch from a mostly rural, agricultural society to an urban, industrial nation.

When the votes were counted, McKinley was the victor, with about 600,000 more votes than Bryan in the popular vote and a margin of 271 to 176 in the Electoral College.

During the election of 1896, McKinley, shown above, conducted a "front porch" campaign from his Canton, Ohio, home. Democratic challenger William Jennings Bryan, in contrast, traveled more than 18,000 miles, sometimes making twenty speeches in a single day.

Garret A. Hobart (1844–99; opposite, top) first entered politics with his election to the New Jersey legislature in 1872. The Republicans chose him as the vice-presidential candidate in hopes of winning New Jersey, which had voted Democratic for much of the nineteenth century.

Puck magazine published this cartoon in 1896, showing Uncle Sam about to paint a group portrait of Ohio-born Republican politicians. Benjamin Harrison appears in the foreground, holding a large hat, and McKinley is dressed as Napoleon, whom cartoonists thought he resembled. John Sherman, McKinley's secretary of state, is dressed as a Puritan (because of his New England heritage). "How did you get in?" is Uncle Sam's question to David P. Hill of New York, who, although a Democrat, supported the Republicans in the 1896 campaign.

"HOW DID YOU GET IN?"

McKINLEY
TAKES OFFICE

McKinley pursued the high-tariff, gold-standard policies he had campaigned on. In 1897, he signed the Dingley Tariff Act into law. The bill raised the tariff rate in general, but lowered it for countries that agreed to reduce their own tariffs on American-made goods. Ironically, the major issue of the election of 1876—the controversy over silver coinage—lost importance not long after McKinley's election. New sources of gold were discovered, increasing the supply of money in circulation in the United States and making credit easier to obtain.

As president, McKinley surprised many of his critics. They had expected the easygoing politician to be controlled by his advisers or to run into problems with Congress. But behind his friendly smile and ready handshake, McKinley had a strong and determined character—although he was always willing to compromise if it would help him achieve his goals. Thanks to his years in the House, he knew how Congress worked, and as president he used this knowledge to his advantage.

In the middle of McKinley's first term, however, his attention shifted from domestic affairs to a pressing foreign-policy problem—Cuba.

Although Mark (Marcus Alonzo) Hanna (1837–1904; left) used his great influence in Republican circles to gain McKinley the presidential nomination, in 1896, he declined a cabinet post offered by a grateful McKinley.

This photograph (below) shows the swearing-in of William McKinley as the nation's twenty-fifth president on March 4, 1897. In his inaugural address, McKinley repeated his belief that a high tariff would help the nation's businesses to recover from the long economic slump.

McKINLEY AND "THE SPLENDID LITTLE WAR"

In 1895, a revolt against Spanish rule began in the countryside of the Caribbean island nation of Cuba. Among Americans, anti-Spanish feeling was whipped up by influential publishers like William Randolph Hearst, whose newspapers exaggerated Spanish cruelty against the Cuban population.

At first, President McKinley resisted calls for American intervention in Cuba. (Assistant Secretary of the Navy Theodore Roosevelt, who wanted the United States to go to war with Spain, reportedly said the president "had no more backbone than a chocolate eclair.") Then, in February 1898, the American warship *Maine* blew up and sank in Havana harbor, killing 266 Americans. The exact cause of the explosion still isn't known, but many Americans assumed a Spanish mine was the cause. American anger at Spain hit the boiling point, and in April, McKinley called on Congress to declare war.

The result was a four-month conflict that Secretary of State John Hay called "the splendid little war." A hastily assembled American army landed in Cuba and quickly defeated the Spanish. The U.S. Navy destroyed one Spanish fleet in Cuba and another in the Spanish-ruled Philippine Islands in the Pacific. American forces also took control of the islands of Puerto Rico in the Caribbean and Guam in the Pacific.

A newspaper cartoon (right) from March 1898 portrays McKinley as an old woman attempting to hold back a tide of congressional and popular pro-war feeling with a broom. By April, McKinley felt he had no choice but to ask for a declaration of war.

This Currier & Ives lithograph (below) shows American warships—products of the naval buildup that began under President Benjamin Harrison—off the Cuban coast. Although the small U.S. Army was poorly prepared for the war, the new, powerful battleships of the navy destroyed Spanish fleets off Cuba and at Manila Bay in the Philippines.

McKINLEY AND THE AMERICAN EMPIRE

With the Spanish-American war over, the United States faced an important decision. What would be done with the territories won from Spain and the millions of people who lived in them? Should they be given their independence and left to rule themselves? Some Americans thought so. A nation that began as a colony and fought to achieve independence had no business colonizing other lands.

But other influential Americans had long believed that the United States, like Britain and other European nations, should build up an empire of overseas colonies. These Americans, called Imperialists, urged McKinley to keep the Philippines, Puerto Rico, and Guam as the basis of an American empire. (Cuba, the cause of the war, received almost complete independence after the end of the conflict.)

The president struggled with the question for several sleepless nights. Finally (he later told a group of clergymen), McKinley decided that granting independence to the Philippines would lead only to "anarchy and misrule." It was the duty of the United States, he believed, to "civilize and Christianize" the islands. (McKinley, who reportedly didn't know where the Philippines were until he looked them up on a globe, seemed unaware that most of the Filipinos were already Christian.) With the president's support, the Philippines were formally annexed to the United States in February 1899.

The United States annexed Hawaii at about the same time it won the Philippines and other possessions from Spain. In 1893, a revolution led by American business people overthrew Queen Liliuokalani (above), the islands' last native monarch.

"I hardly know which to take first!" says Uncle Sam in the cartoon shown here (right), as he studies a menu listing Cuba, Puerto Rico, the Philippines, and the Sandwich Islands (an old name for Hawaii). President McKinley, in a waiter's apron, looks on with approval.

John Hay (1838–1905; right) was appointed secretary of state by McKinley in April 1898. Hay was an able diplomat who strongly supported McKinley's policies in the Philippines and elsewhere. In 1899, he extended the United States' worldwide influence by issuing the Open Door notes, diplomatic letters that pledged American support for China's independence.

WELL, I HARDLY KNOW WHICH TO TAKE FIRST!

McKINLEY: REELECTION AND ASSASSINATION

Even before the signing of the annexation treaty, armed Filipinos—who wanted independence, not just a change from Spanish to American rule—began fighting U.S. forces in the Philippines. The conflict turned into a bitter guerrilla war, with many deaths and acts of cruelty on both sides. The "Philippine Insurrection," as it was called, was one of the major issues of the election of 1900.

Once again, the Democratic nominee was William Jennings Bryan, who opposed McKinley's policies in the Philippines and American imperialism in general. McKinley easily won the Republican nomination, with a war hero, Theodore Roosevelt, as his running mate. The Republicans downplayed the issue of the Philippines, pointing instead to the renewed prosperity of McKinley's first term and promising more of the same. As in 1896, McKinley easily defeated Bryan.

On September 6, 1901, the president arrived at a speaking engagement in Buffalo, New York. McKinley was shaking hands when a man carrying a handkerchief appeared in the receiving line. The man was Leon Czolgosz, an anarchist (someone who doesn't believe in government of any kind), and the handkerchief concealed a gun. Czolgosz shot McKinley twice before horrified onlookers wrestled him to the floor. The president clung to life for nine days, finally dying on September 14. He was fifty-eight years old.

President William McKinley is shown (right) arriving at the Pan-American Exposition in Buffalo, New York, on September 6, 1901. (The exposition showcased the products and cultures of North and South America.) McKinley's secretary George Cortelyou feared an attack on the president.

A horrified crowd looks on (below) as Leon Czolgosz shoots the president at the Pan-American Exposition in Buffalo, on September 6, 1901. Despite the pain of his wounds, McKinley's first words following the shooting expressed concern for Czolgosz. "Don't let them hurt him," the president gasped as onlookers tackled the assassin. Czolgosz was electrocuted six weeks later.

Resource Guide

Key to picture positions: (T) top, (C) center, (B) bottom; and in combinations: (TL) top left, (TR) top right, (BL) bottom left, (BR) bottom right, (RC) right center, (LC) left center.
Key to picture locations within the Library of Congress collections (and where available, photo negative numbers): P - Prints and Photographs Division; R - Rare Book Division; G - General Collections; MSS - Manuscript Division; G&M - Geography Division
Other sources: AC - Architect of the Capitol; BHL - Benjamin Harrison Library; USGS - U.S. Geological Survey

PICTURES IN THIS VOLUME

2–3 Washington, D.C., P **4–5** Bryan poster, P, USZC4-824 **6–7** Washington Monument, P **8–9** Map, USGS

Timeline: **10–11** demonstration, P, USZ62-27754; Clara Barton, P, USZ62-19319 **12–13** parade, P; riot, P **14–15** settlers camp, P, USZ62-847; bicycle, G **16–17** Bryan poster, P, USZ62-30770; gold rush, P, USZ62-48136

Part I: **18–19** cartoon, P, USZC2-1239 **20–21** TL, Lucy Hayes, P, USZ62-5491; BR, birthplace, P, USZ62-32446; TR, family, P, LC-BH832-2028 **22–23** TR, Hayes, P, USZ62-19864; C, battle, P, USZ62-12926 **24–25** TR, poster, P; BR, house, P, USZ62-1826; TR, poster, P **26–27** Electoral Commission, AC **28–29** TL, candlelight session, P, USZ62-97512; TR, cartoon, P, USZ62-34364; BR, Tilden, P **30–31** TL, Hayes w/wife, P; cartoon, G **32-33** TL, clambake, P, USZ62-7597; C, strike, G **34–35** TR, birthplace, P, USZ62-5624; TL, Lucretia Garfield, P, USZ62-2573 **36–37** TL, Garfield, P, LC BH82-3820; TR, family, P, USZ62-14096; BR, battle, P **38–39** TL, Hancock, P; TR, cartoon, P, USZ62-4915; BR, diary, MSS **40–41** assassination, P, USZ62-12825 **42–43** TL, Guiteau, G; BL, Garfield, G; TR, prisoner, G; BR, crazy Guiteau, G **44–45** TL, wife, USZ62-25794; BR, Broadway, P, USZ62-4885; TR, Arthur, P **46–47** C, Wall Street, P, USZ62-13201; TL, daughter, P, USZ62-98155 **48–49** Arthur, P,

USZ62-60395; BR, cartoon, P **50–51** C, picnic, P, USZ62-24823; BR, cartoon, P, USZ62-50177 **52–53** C, Buffalo, G; TL, sister, P, USZ62-25796 **54–55** BR, trains, G; TR, Cleveland, P **56–57** TL, baby cartoon, P, USZ62-34246; BL, celebration, P **58–59** TL, Frances Cleveland, P, USZ62-25797; TR, wedding, G; BR, cartoon, P

Part II: **60–61** parade, P, USZC4-824 **62–63** BR, school notes, MSS; TR, birthplace, P, USZ62-7610; TL, Caroline Harrison, P, USZ62-25798 **64–65** TR, Gen'l Harrison, BHL; C, troop, P **66–67** TL, Morton, P, USZ61-441; BR, music cover, MSS; TR, family, P, USZ62-103992 **68–69** BR, Mary Harrison, P, USZ62-25800; BL, cartoon, P, USZ62-792; TR, house, P **70–71** TR, ideas, G; BR, "On Deck" cartoon, P, USZ62-9651 **72–73** C, Cherokee Strip, P; TR, Mrs. Cleveland, P **74–75** TL, strike, P, USZ62-3526; TR, *Puck* cover, P; BR, house, G **76–77** TR, family, P, USZ62-28395; C, cartoon, P **78–79** TR, birthplace, P, USZ62-32661; C, battle, P **80–81** C, bowling cartoon, P; TL, Ida McKinley, P, USZ62-25801 **82–83** C, cartoon, P; TL, Bryan, P **84–85** TL, McKinley, P, USZ62-83820; TR, Hobart, P, USZ62-49957; BR, cartoon, P **86–87** C, inaugural, P; TL, Hanna, P, USZ62-24153 **88–89** TR, cartoon, P; C, ships, P **90–91** TL, Queen Lili, P, USZ62-22488; BR, cartoon, P, USZ62-91465; TR, Hay, P, USZ62-7222 **92–93** TR, McKinley, P; C, assassination, P, USZ62-5377

SUGGESTED READING

BLASSINGAME, WYATT. *The Look-It-Up Book of Presidents.* New York: Random House, 1984
BOARDMAN, F. W., JR. *America and the Gilded Age, 1876–1900.* New York: Henry Z. Walck, 1972
DEGREGORIO, W. A. *The Complete Book of U.S. Presidents.* New York: Dembner Books, 1991.

GOULD, LEWIS, L. *The Presidency of William McKinley.* Lawrence: University Press of Kansas,1981
WHITNEY, D. C. *The American Presidents,* 6th ed. New York: Doubleday, 1986.

Index

Page numbers in *italics* indicate illustrations